BEAR STARE POETRY

JACKSON DUROCHER

Bear Stare Poetry

JACKSON DUROCHER

Copyright © 2025 by Jackson Durocher.

All rights reserved. No part of this book may be reproduced in any form or by any electronic or mechanical means, including information storage and retrieval systems, without permission in writing from the publisher, except by reviewers, who may quote brief passages in a review.

MILTON & HUGO L.L.C.
4407 Park Ave., Suite 5
Union City, NJ 07087, USA

Website: www. miltonandhugo.com
Hotline: 1- 888-778-0033
Email: info@miltonandhugo.com

Ordering Information:
Quantity sales. Special discounts are available on quantity purchases by corporations, associations, and others. For details, contact the publisher at the address above.

Library of Congress Control Number: 2025915238
ISBN-13:   979-8-89285-600-3   [Paperback Edition]
            979-8-89285-601-0   [Digital Edition]

Rev. date: 07/22/2025

Dedicated to the ones
I love and whom love me
In return

You gotta look inside yourself and say, "What
am I willing to put up with today?
Not fucking this.

-Arin Hanson (2012)

Table of Contents

"Drive" 1
"Goodbye" 2
"Actor" 3
"New Years" 5
"Melodic Isolation" 6
"Serenity" 8
"Wanderer" 9
"Lie" 11
"Pissed Off Puppy" 12
"Addicted to Shame" 14
"Convict" 15
"Proposal" 17
"Drag" 18
"Affair" 20
"Song" 21
"Sicily" 23
"Dancing in the Snow" 24
"Tinder" 26
"Noh" 27
"Slumber" 29
"Yellow Girl, Young Canary" 30
"Item" 32
"School Girl" 33
"Lonely" 36
"Young Maid" 38
"Beggar" 47

"The Cave" 49
"Rest in Peace" 51
"Little Miss White" 52
"Perfect Body" 55
"Behind the Scenes" 57
"Update to the Simulation" 60
"Regret" 61
"Flower Girl Red" 62
"Friends Held Dear" 64
"Lighter" 66
"Tortured Princess" 67
"Josee" 70
"Broadmoor Masquerade" 72
"Lute" 74
"Malaysia" 77
"Ryu Murakami" 78
"A Woman in Venice" 79
"Puppeteer" 81
"Sore Eyes" 82
"Portrait of a Poet" 83
"Best in Show" 85
"Revolution Poem" 86
"The Gardener" 87
"Ocarina" 92
"Truth or Dare" 94
"Study of a Model" 96
"The Dancer" 99
"Bitch Please" 103
"Another Hug" 104
"Stranger" 107
"Family" 109
"Goodbye, My Love, Goodbye" 111
"Persuasion" 114
"Boy in the Red Vest" 116

"Neon" 120
"Totoro" 122
"Sleeping Mother" 124
"Hades and Persephone" 126
"Kings Bride" 127
"A Portrait of a Daughter" 129
"New Orleans" 133
"The Animals and the Girl" 136
"Ocean of Words" 139
"Self-love Discovered" 140

Afterword 142
About the Author 143

"Drive"

I drive the winding road of Santa Fe,
My son in the passenger ,
Pointing at each tree
Every beach
And all the strange clouds
Shaping imagination
I watch in humour as he explains
That tree is breathing
That beach is speaking Mandarin
Those clouds look like Pandas.
There's houses in the distance
We traverse with speed
Every house is a story
Every person holds some lore
That house is haunted
That house is singing
That man has a secret
That woman stole his heart.
We continue on our journey
Mine at the wheel
His making imagination real
I raised a poet of reality.

"Goodbye"

Come to the foyer,
Where we may say goodbye.
Though you despise that word;
"Goodbye" meaning forever.

You'd rather I say "later"
But you married an asshole
Who goes for a rise
And always says "Goodbye."

You know I jest
I love you above all the rest
And a smile I feel when
Greetings come

Goodbye little darling
Love you honeybee
Goodbye or later
I'll see you oh so soon.

"Actor"

123 breathe
Curtains open
On Cisarro
In the land of Mexico.

Trying to portray
What a buzzed man wrote
High off of cigarette smoke
But Bullshit is what it is.

He tries to emanate
A man of conviction
Blamed of stealing a coin or two
Then it happens.

His mouth is silent,
His arms are talking,
Heads gone,
Fingers play the song.

He waves around while crowd cheer,
Unaware,
Or ignorante,
The actor without a head.

Many believe it to be stage magic,
Until Cisarro hits the floor,
who can breathe without some lips
And now the arms are limp.

A story of the ages,
A Shakespearean plot,
A man of artistic squalor,
A death of possibilities.

To be or not to be,
That is the question.

Jackson Durocher

"New Years"

I am handed champagne
At a New Years party
Unable to recollect why
This stranger likes me.

It's a lindy hop party
And a new one came to play
Though somehow she follows
My lackluster ways.

I'm not a bad dancer
I think myself talented
But the cheap booze
And blues moves me away.

I take her hand in mine
As we jazz our bodies astray
Not remembering who
Was playing the lead.

Though I never got a number
I hold her true in ways non-physical
A memory of a dancer
A Mary of my day.

"Melodic Isolation"

Cling of the string
Clang of a pedal
I sit in desolation
Playing my melody
Dolly left with Richard
While voicing her disdain
I'm half the man her lover is
And I'm half the man I used to be.
I play in Piano
Dotting the keys
With unforeseen
Possibilities
Thought grows
And my fingers hit hard
I raise in tone
And my feeling scorn.
I write my music
And hum my numbness
In melodic isolation.

"SERENITY"

A hand upon a doorknob
I turn it to serenity
A room most warm
With books on books & art on walls.

The colour of wallpaper
Bleak, with floors dull
Though basic makes beauty
And extreme creates insane.

So even when it's boring
I find it to be warm
My room I call "serenity"
A Joseph to my name.

"Wanderer"

Unparalleled Decisions
And lack luster choices
Have left me with a few dimes
And an unknown pain in my shoulder.

I've been banished from prior shelters
Sentenced to wander dampened streets
With unreliable companions
Who'd sooner slash me before lending a hand.

I pass a dirty beggar playing an untuned guitar
With a missing G string and voice cracked & cold.
Knowing he'd use all busked coins for cheap booze
I give up my dimes.

He saluted me & I nod back
"Amen brother," I think.
I trod on in this endless night
Trying for shelter in the form of an underpass.

May my decent beggar deed be repaid
Even though I know my prayer is shit.

"Don't make me repeat myself,
It's embarrassing."
Though she insists
I utter those words once more.
"You were right."

"LIE"

I am a poet,
A beggar,
And an asshole.

I write experiences
And make believe.

I tell lore to behold
And lies to deny responsibility.

I wish I was an
Honest man
But fiction is easier.

I'd rather hide behind a mask
Then show a cracked face.

May I hide
Forevermore

"Pissed Off Puppy"

Pissed off puppy
A dog of rage
No treats today
No need to behave.

The streets will
Flow with chaos.

Pissed off puppy,
No walkies today,
No toys to play,
Vengeance will show.

Through sheer force of will,
And there will be blood.

Pissed off puppy,
The dog who won't be swayed,
Pissed off puppy,
Todays is the owners last.

"Addicted to Shame"

I haven't a clue
What I'll finish first
The book,
Or the bottle.

But I do know,
I am addicted to shame.

I'd rather be a fool
And have fun,
Than be
Bored and responsible.

I know I am an adult
Though I am a hypocrite by trade.

"Convict"

A man sits in dress,
Awaits his address,
From judge and jury
Of this unknown trial.

He ponders what he's done
For his crime is unknown
Like Kafka's famous trial,
Everyone is living in denial.

"Why god?
Why must I suffer,
Slings and arrows of
Verbal aggression?"

He turns his head upwards
And stares at a jail light.
A fly flies around in circle
Unaware of the futile
Meaninglessness he exhibits.

"Why can't I be the fly?
Why can't I fly nowhere,
And be content with that?"
He curses but it won't do much.

A guard knocks on the bars
And calls for him to follow
Though he walks him past
The courtroom and into the
Gallows square of burdened sin.

"You have been sentenced
To die by the hanging of Gallows
Any words before you dangle?"
"No, except why was I senten…"

He pulled the lever before
He spoke. the convict, the dead
Will never know why
In this cruel world of the unknown,
Why was he sent to hang.

"Proposal"

On one knee
With my fiance to be
I ask her to marry me.

She stares in confusion,
Than replies "Why not"
"Though I wish you had picked a better ring."

A ring pop in hand
I promise one better
Though I can only afford
An arcade spider ring.

Beggars can't be choosers.

"Drag"

I drag a cigarette
And sip my bourbon,
While this scholar sits
And hollers squalor.

I tell him to drink,
His throat is dry.
So he sips his liquor
And the burn shuts his trap.

"Now speak your point.
We have bourbon
To drink so no need
For whines."

He slanders sin
On the friends
Brave enough to
Confess his work is shit.

Though I'm not as courageous
So my lips stay sealed
Allowing him the compliments
He keenly fishes for.

"Bastards are what they are!
But you understand."
I take a gulp
To bottle my contradictions.

I've read the novels,
I've read his poems,
Purely all hallmark films
And human AI's commonality.

I finish my drink
And hail a cab,
For I no longer wish
To deal with drag.

"Affair"

She wants security,
He wants a body.

She needs loyalty,
He hates restrictions.

While tending to their child,
He is wild in bed.

Not with the Mother,
But with another.

She gives him papers,
He will not sign.

For where may a broke man sleep,
Without a couch and landlord's suite.

No longer a wife,
Just a roommate.

She always play Mother,
While he denies "Father."

"Song"

Guity fingers pluck string
While a lost pianist
Try to follow my
Uneven beat.

I make up a story
Always involving 'pain'
Even though I'm well off
And not a beggar by trade.

No one wants to hear
About a middle class
Curly haired poet
Trying to sound 'different.'

I am a liar
And a coward
But hey,
I do rhyme well.

"Sicily"

I sit on the steps
Leading to the sea,
Dreaming of the lady
I wish so much to see.

Hair of golden curls,
Lying in the sand,
On a beach down in Sicily,
where I'll never be her man.

She's always with another,
A new one every week,
For love is just a word
And survival demands security.

For those with empty wallets,
Are the homeless ones with tans.

"Dancing in the Snow"

Snowflakes fall and melt
on the tongue of the man
Who sticks it out towards
A girl who is most sweet.

She returns the flesh
Sticking through lips
then he extends a hand
To which she accepts.

Dancing in the snow
Like two melting snowflakes
Hot at the touch in weather
Most cold.

Dancing with the snowflakes
Since no one is here
He holds her
And she holds him

Dancing in the cold breeze
Where only her he sees
Only love in cold freeze
And cheeks red from cold

Fox trouting in cold frost

A dancing couple lost in thought
A man in the eyes of a lover
And a girl in warmth like a fire

Dancing in the snow
Are the boy and girl.
Jack frost and Milly Chilly,
The coldest touch with the warmest heart.

May they dance forevermore,
In the coldest night,
In the warmest eyes,
In the whitest snow.

"Tinder"

Right
Left
Left
Right

Match
Her name is Marie
Her Bio;
A song

"You see trees of green,
Red roses too,
The pearl of your eye,
And me with you.
So you think to yourself,
What a wonderful girl."

"Cute," I think as I
bounce back a response.

"I see skies of blue,
And clouds of white.
The bright blessed day,
And a date tonight.
So I think to myself,
Maybe dinner for two?"

Jackson Durocher

"Noh"

Haanya dances
upon the stage,
Clad in mask
Of demon bains.

Jealous she is,
Possessed? could be.
Though warranted agreed,
Upon the stage.

A man has left
With maid in tow,
For eloping is so simple
When partners on death's door.

But, Miraculously healed
From ailments tight hold.
She pursues the bastard
In traditional dance form.

A ballet of the broken,
A pirouette of scorn,
A Noh play of pain,
A Noh show of strength.

But when faced with fate,
When arriving at the gate,
Of her old sick husband,
Who passed without goodbye.

The chambermaid sits grieving
As she hands the ex a sheet,
Of apologies of the broken,
Apologies not enough.

"SLUMBER"

I long for slumber
And I don't mean death.
I wish to be curled
Asleep in bed.

When choices become burdens
And people love to fight.
You pray to angels,
To create the night.

Now so long everyone
I got my jammies on.
It's bedtime for the broken,
They are chewing melatonin.

"Yellow Girl, Young Canary"

A yellow girl
Feeds canary
A shroom picked
And gobbled quick.

Found with broken wing
Upon backyard doorsteps,
A young girl nurses
A bird so weak.

She wears a yellow frock,
Same shade as the birdie,
Two bright colours
Glowing happiness.

She keeps him in a
Milk crate,
And feeds him everyday
for soon, he will fly, fly away.

A good two month go by
And birdie now may try
Time to say goodbye,
To young canary yellow.

She lets a teardrop fall,

For she hates a sad farewell,
But she is happy for her birdie.
May you defend your wing my friend.

"ITEM"

I stare at the phone
and people who once
Saw great beauty in me
Though it was another instead

I was only a lover,
But they love her,
And never the item,
The one named "Jackson."

Now I sit sipping
Cold ice water,
Sobering my tears
From loneliness and not a bottle.

"School Girl"

A young girl walks to school
Down cherry lanes
Of blackened Spain.

It is 6 in the morning,
With class starting at 8.
She leaves quite early
So she is not late.

She lives far from the only school,
An old brick building
Which survived the war.

Cold summer morning
After last nights downpour.
The streets glistens in the light
Of the moon.

Skipping down the lanes of houses
And trees withering in autumn breeze,
A smiles comes wide between cheeks.

Last school day, a girl smiled her way,
She was cute and petite,
And she thinks they might work.

Ma and Pa are old fashioned
But so is everyone,
Because I will sooner be married
To a man than a girl I find rather grand.

The school girl ponders,
why she is strange,
Why she is gay,
Why she can't?

The 50's aren't kind,
The 50's are unfair,
To the girl who loves,
The one born the same.

One day she prays
She can runaway,
With the cute petite girl
That smiled her way.

There is an hour left
Of her trek to school
She has lots of time
To ponder a crime.

The crime of love
For the queer like her
She wishes to appeal
The law that denied her feelings.

"Lonely"

I am lonely
In forced isolation.
As poems are written
In busy bars with music
That will cripple.

I wander Whyte Ave
Searching for some reasons
That will define myself
As something that's not
A broken man.

It's four in the morning,
I work at seven.
Though I must walk on,
For if I stop,
Then who am I?

A poet of dissolution,
A jester and a con,
A con to myself,
And the broken heart
I lay to thee.

May I find a home,
Somewhere to lie down,
Where burden can unload,
And I can disappear,
From all fear.

"Young Maid"

Young maid,
Young girl,
Young helper,
Young soul,

Hired to be
A chambermaid
To the young master
Sick in bed.

Can't raise a finger,
Can't turn his eyes,
Just can sense a presence
Who's only the maid.

The mother is in the parlor,
The father is at the table,
The brothers off at war,
And the boy is all alone.

Young maid sits with
The sicken boy reading
Books like "Jane Eyre"
To dispel all fear.

Young maid is given a
Bed in the corner,
Just a simple pillow and
Blanket on the cold hard floor.

She does not mind,
She does not care,
It is better than the
Workhouse from days before.

She grows fond of
The master, even without
A word, a presence of a
Friend, never before had.

One night, he spoke
Soft, cracked, croaked,
A 'thank you' and a finger
Beckoning an ear.

She shuffled forward,
And bent down to hear.
He told her "You're pretty,"
Then fell back to slumber.

She remained by his side,
Holding his hand dear.
She thought herself plain,
She has never blushed before.

No one came the next day,
Nor the next,
Not even a week later,
No one visited the boy.

The maid fed him porridge,
Wiped his brow,
Massaged his hands,
And read him aloud.

She was rewarded,
Each night a 'thank you'
And a call for an ear.
She always looked forward to it.

He got better soon,
Still bed ridden,
But hands would twitch,
Eyes met hers.

Periodically he smiled,
Just fleetingly,
But that was enough
For her hard work.

Three days go by,
He speaks more clear,
Speaks more sincere.

The maid sits with him,
And reads him 'persuasion.'
He listens though eyes
Her curiously.

She pretends not to notice
But he speaks to her.
Clear and sweet
"What's your name?"

"What?" she voiced confused.
"What's your name?"
"I don't have one."
Silence filled the room.

"The workhouse called me 'runt.'"
Silence again then softly he spoke
"You are now Ann, like this book."
"Okay."

The maid kept reading,
Unable to voice some words,
Especially Miss Elliots,
She blushed again.

Winter soon came and
The room grew cold,
Especially the floor,
The cold hard floor.

Shivered and quaked under
Blankets and shake.
Unable to sleep,
Not even a peep.

The master noticed, Even
When weak, he tried to speak,
But the cold proved difficult.
"Come," was all he mustered.

The maid shuffled
Cold and weary,
And lent an ear to
The master.

"In" spoke softly through lips,
He motioned weakly to the bed.
"No, I cannot, it goes against order."
"In…please."

She thought,
She stewed,
Deep in wonder and
Soon she got under.

Warmth enveloped her
And she never felt more
Comfort than the masters
Bed. soft, warm, complete.

An arm wrapped around
Her waist, and now she faced
The boy who stared with grace
Of what he calls 'beautiful.'

"Sir, your hands…are cold."
"So are you…my darling."
"I…don't know…what to do?"
"Just hold me, please."

A night most sweet
On a cold November evening
Two souls from different worlds
Share love most warmly.

Waking up in lovers embrace
The two face a figure
Of beauty's grace.
An everlasting bond.

Jackson Durocher

Holding each other
In a bed called 'home.'
The mother came in,
She saw what she calls sin.

"You bitch! I gave you shelter,
I gave you work! And you
Seduce a sick dying boy!
Get out of here Harlot!"

She tried to defend,
She tried to persuade,
She tried everything,
Though to explain did not do.

"Alright, ma'am.
I am sorry."
Head hung low,
She prepared to go.

"Wait, no, why go?"
The maid turned to see
The boy staring, smiling
And now he faced his mother.

"We are to be wed,
Aren't we Ann?"
She smiled through tears confused,
'Why? Why for me?'

The mother tried to object
Though shut by
The twitching hand
Raised in 'silence'

"Mother, mom,
You left me,
You and father,
never came, not once."

The boy knew
He was sentenced death,
Alone in bed with a
Maid for accountability.

But he lives and
Fortune now his,
Being 18 and a grandfathers
Favored grandson.

A will for him,
A fortune his,
As long as he lives;
Unless dead does he lose.

The master pulls bed covers
And stands with weakened legs.
He walks to Ann and
Stands with his bride.

"Mother, gather Father;
You no longer belong here.
There is a townhouse near
For you, to be clear.

Objections given,
All denied so
The master walks
To the telephone.

Jackson Durocher

"You have 5 seconds
For verbal comply
Before I phone
For removal."

A huff and puff
And now she's off,
For stuff of hers
And father in tow.

"Ann, Darling,
Will you marry me?"
Tears dot the floor with
Blushed cheeks, "yes."

A week passes,
The house is clear,
And two lovers
Share a kiss so warm.

A reception in bed,
For two newlyweds.
A quick engagement
With no need for glamour.

Man and wife,
A master not sick
And a maid who loves
And is loved in return.

"The Young Maid"

"Beggar"

You once said you'd fight
For love or something you can
Laugh about but now you
Do not feel so loving, do ya?

It's hard to try to hold some care
for someone who is caring for another,
Someone who is leaving you to suffer.

So walking empty streets, you think
Maybe he's no Mr Darcy,
Maybe he's a beggar.
Maybe he's a beggar who had
Stole himself a suit to trick
A little girl like you.

Maybe he sang lullabies
To lull, you' girl to sleep so later he
Can find another one to use.
This beggar of infidelity,
Tricking all the taken
To be mistaken.

You try to confront this man who
Tricked you into feeling sad,
Like Eve in the land of Eden,
Like a snake tricking you to suffer,
Tricking you to eat the apple of Eden.

So maybe he's a beggar.
Maybe he's a beggar who could
Only find a place to sleep by
Singing words he did not mean.

There's differences in tones when
Saying a word like "Love."
A word is a words and
The person makes it true.

I can promise you I am no bird,
But I can lie and say I fly
Above chimney tops,
Like a singing meadowlark.

So maybe this beggar man knew to
Say a little lie to get a roof
Above his head and shelter,
For when closing yourself off to love
It's easy to trick someone who hasn't.

So maybe he's a beggar who leaves
A trail of broken women anywhere he travels
Maybe he's a beggar,
And always a beggar.

"The Cave"

She isolated herself in
A cave at the peak.
Where she longs to be,
Alone and desolate.

I climb the mountain
And enter her abode,
Where I call out emotions
Though she only sinks deeper.

I try to fix what is broken
But she only slides further,
In the crevices
Of wet rock.

So I sit down,
Cross my legs
And wait,
In pure silence.

For she comes out
And sits with me,
In utter quiet,
Where presence is key.

I wait and wait
Then she speaks,
Like a faucet,
It all comes pouring out.

I nod
And listen,
While agreeing
That does sound tough.

Slowly we stand,
And she vents,
As we walk out the cave
And down the peak.

She only needed to speak,
And not be taught.
To solve a problem,
Is to listen. Nothing more.

"Rest in Peace"

Kill me softly,
Lay me down,
Upon the grass,
Up on a hill.

Where bluejay's die,
And the reaper cries.
Please read this poem
Upon the grave:

"Sing the hero a graceful ballad,

And tuck the villain swiftly to bed.
The man who lies, was
The Yin and Yang.

A good man with slight evil
And a bastard playing friend.
No good without evil,
And no evil without love.

Rest in peace Mr Lynch,
May the white lodge be serenity.

(David Lynch)
Rest in peace
(1946-2025)

"Little Miss White"

I am awakened by a voice
Asking to spend a night,
For the dark is cold,
And the stars are out.

I awake to see a little girl
In a dress of white.
Standing most frail
By my bed pale.

I ask how she got here?
so she motions to the door.
"It was unlocked and a candle lit."
'Idiot,' I think, though that sinks.

"What's your name?"
She shrugs then mutters
"Call me Little Miss White,"
Then silence takes hold.

Alright…okay…I guess you can stay
As long as you behave.
I do not want a roommate,
But tonight will be okay.

She smiles and hops
Under my covers
And before I can exclaim 'hey!'
She falls deep, deep asleep.
Soft rises come from her chest,
And hair of auburn fall across
My pillow case.
She is cute, like a baby.

So I crawl out of bed
And sleep in my rocking chair
That will be okay tonight and
I fell asleep quickly and nice.

When rooster cries,
And I arise from a slumber of peace
And face completes the scene,
Of poetic moves.

She waves and yips 'hey!"
As I see she has been singing
A tune of melodic dissonance,
And keys are sharp when flat.

"You're still here?"
"Yup, fed and ready"
"Good, nice" and I sigh
Why do I not say 'goodbye?'

"How old are you?"
"9 and three quarters."
"So young huh…Well you
Better stay here then."

She cocks her head
And stare bewildered.
"You are too young for begging
And not street safe."

"I can stay?"
"As long as you behave."
Her wraps wrap around me,
In her white silk frock.

A stranger before,
A friend today,
A daughter for now,
And a vow forever.

"Perfect Body"

Come to the sofa,
I want to feel your hair.
Soft strands upon my hand,
A dark shade with hues so warm.

You gifted me a mandolin
With lacquered oak clear.
Polished with a brush,
You sang and I blushed.

I pluck the strings,
You match each ring,
And sing we shall
And sing we must.

I see great honour
Behind your green eyes,
With little speckled black around
An iris small but strong.

Caress me with your naked hand,
Please let me feel your touch,
For even without lotion on,
Your skin feel soft and lush.

Walk me to the bus station,
Where we match our
Steps in time,
Steps in union.

Kiss me with lipstick on,
Or dry and bare and rough,
For nothing can change
The way I feel your gentle touch.

Perfection in realism
And darling your whole ,
In the eyes of me,
And the eyes of the creator.

"Behind the Scenes"

Behind the scenes
Of each of the acts
Marquo flirts with
Benidette, the leading dancer.

She plays hard and he
Doesn't catch on for
She is engaged, and
Soon to be wed.

Simon, the curtain boy
Asked her a fortnight ago,
On one knee, they vowed
To flee, after what now plays.

Someone is a nark though
And whispers get around for
When curtain bow arrives,
The coach does not.

Instead, Marquo shows
With a pistol in hand,
For riches should
Out-buy love.

Simon attempts to
Wrestle the gun,
But a pop and bang
Proves it futile.

Marquo never truly
Meant to kill,
Only scare but now
He flees in fear instead.

Benidette is left
To grieve the death
Of Simon and
The death of love.

Like Romeo and Juliet,
Love never dies,
But people do;
She will join him soon.

"Update to the Simulation"

Update to the simulation:
The earth is round;
Not flat anymore.
Apologies to flat earthers
But times are changing.

"Regret"

Does death cry when
An angel dies and
No ones there to weep?

Do parents regret a
Word or two,
Spoken to the baby?

Does the owner wish
They spoke of bliss and
Not verbal whips at the dog?

One may wish,
And still hold regrets.

We are only human,

Aren't we?

"Flower Girl Red"

Deep in a meadow,
A girl picks flower,
Dressed in red
From head to toe.

She pretends to be
A princess lost,
Far from her kingdom
Of long ago lore.

She picks the lilacs
And tulips in bunches,
And weaves herself
A flower crown so pretty.

Prancing and dancing
Around the grass.
She is the princess
Of nature's kingdom.

The flower girl red,
The princess of natural earth.

Jackson Durocher

"Friends Held Dear"

Last night,
I sat with my friends
held dear.

When a game,
Switched to stories,
Of lore and scorn,
We sat, we listened
We shared a tear.

To what shaped
Our journeys.
What brought us here.

In this quaint
Little room,
This warmth of
Possibility.

I can speak of sin
I can talk of 'the dirty,'
But why stay shackled,
When other inmates are pretty.

Why weep the pain
Of a storage closet,
Why weep the shame
Of a panic attack.

When I share space
And respect takes place,
With my friends held dear,
My un-blooded family.
May we thrive forevermore.
To us,
The unfiltered freaks.

"LIGHTER"

I carry around a lighter,
Though I do not smoke.
It plays the spark
For those whose damned
And desperate for some bitter sweet
Relief through its fuel.

"Do you have a light?"
"Yes I do!"
"Care to smoke?"
"Nah, I'm good; but tell me
About your blues?"

"Tortured Princess"

It's 2 am,
I'm trying to sleep,
But there's a young girl
Staring right at me,
She calls herself the tortured princess.

She tells me of unholy beats,
And drunken stupors of defeat,
Which led her next to my bedside.

I ask her,
"What is wrong my dear?
How may I bring up the cheer?"
Though she only whispers,
"You will never know."

Because How many times can she survive,
When everyone longs for her defeat?

Because How many times will she survive,
When people want to lock her body away?

She asks me if she can sit down,
So I pat the bed and whisper "yes"

So she slides her thin frame right in.

She wraps a hand around my wrist
and slowly draws in for a kiss.

Since that is one way to remain alive.

Because How many times can she survive,
When people see a face and not a soul?
Because How many times will she survive,
When she has to stay 10 moves ahead?

I tell her you don't have to kiss,
For I'm no master to his miss,
I'm just a humble broker for her.

She states I am the lucky duck,
For pressing forward on my luck,
And meeting someone so fragile but pure.

Now I hope that she'll survive,
Because now she resides in my mind.

Now I know that she'll survive,
Now no long tortured and just a simple girl.

A day ago she appeared to me,
Lashed and scorned,
And wet from cold,
Asking "please,
May I have a bed."

I wave her in but she collapses at my feet,

Exhausted,
Sickened,
Horrified,
And weary.

So I carried her to my guest bed
And I sit with her a bit,
Until she is all dry,
Until there is no cry.

I go to bed and that's where we begin,
At 2 am,
At my bedside.

The tortured princess,
Not anymore.

"Josee"

They are after you Josee,
They'll hang you up to dry.

Run away Josee,
Run away and hide.

Don't make a sound Josee,
Don't even make a sigh.

That man Josee,
That guy.

The one you had denied,
He didn't take it well Josee.

He took it like a man,
A fragile masculine man.

He did not like the 'no,'
He took it to the core.

He could have anyone,
But he couldn't have you.

Why are men like that Josee?
Why are some depraved?

Are you okay Josee?
Are you feeling safe?

Are you there Josee?
Josee, are you there?

Josee?
Josee?

"Broadmoor Masquerade"

Dawned incognito,
A hotel Masquerade,
A halloween Party,
Whose host I hadn't known.

That friday morning,
I received an unsigned letter,
A mask of whitest white with
Two black circles around the eyes.

I haven't a clue why I came,
But seeing a figure
With a mask the same,
I decide to stay anyway.

A body of the past,
But only a reminder,
For who lied under that
Miracle mask was not
An acquaintance from days before.

The past is the past,
Tomorrow is unknown,
So I shall make her the present.

I take her to the suite

Where lovers lie,
And create a prophecy
Of days of bliss.

I shall make her holy,
Make her the gift,
For even in the present,
I see the angelic future.

"Lute"

A lute
Was all
That was in my
Husbands will.

A lute of oak
With a rough face
And strings thin,
Why this? Why a lute?

A lute won't raise kids,
A lute won't pay bills,
A lute won't help when the
Rent collectors come due.

This man, this Bastard,
My husband thought
Not to give us money?
Or something to be kind?

I stare at this lute
And see between the strings,
In the hollow cave of the oak
There's a note poking through.

I shake it out and
pray it has some use,
Then read and read,
Till tears come flowing.

"My love Marianne,
The light of past life,
I am sorry to leave you
Widowed and strife."
"My wife Marianne,
I leave you my lute,
Pawn it or keep it;
It's yours to choose."

"My eternal Marianne,
I gave it for reminder
Of the music you created
When I looked into your eyes."

"My only Marianna,
I'm sorry I have left,
Tell the kids I love them,
I know I will always love you."

I hold the lute close,
Pressing tight against bosom,
I weep and weep,
And a promise mine.

I'll hold the lute
Close when needed,
When needing reminders
Of the one who keeps the flame lit.

I'll miss you forever honey,
My eternal melody.

"Malaysia"

At a concert hall in Malaysia,
Where a woman stands fair and true,
Her voices spoken to masses
And a mouth with countless reviews.

She soars among angels,
Though lies in beds of pleasure,
For like Eve sinned in Eden,
Where she could've been among power.

Now plummeting to the floor
After scandal reports take page,
She drowns herself in sorrow,
For booze can hide all tears.

Now just a common lady
After the stage doors been closed,
No longer in the concert hall,
No longer among the music.

She wanders though not lost,
For she knows she has no home,
For stripped from all her beauty,
She's now a woman like the others.

"Ryu Murakami"

Piercing deep within flesh so warm.
An author I fancy writes a plot,
Psycho and scorning,
Warning of story.

A child in a locker,
A widow and a movie,
A banished sinful nature,
And addiction so clear.

To bathe in uncomfort,
To swim among sharks
As a minnow in a pool,
Where discovery is fear.

So take a little chance,
Dip a single toe,
In the world of Murakami,
A poet of the torn.

"A Woman in Venice"

A street in Venice
Where a woman walks,
Silent and cold but
Confident in step.

She plays sincere and
Full of beauty,
As people watch,
And people stare.

A bow in hair
But torn shawl,
Covering blouse small
And skirt long.

A gypse and past lover,
A woman and a scholar,
For she can tell people
Better than you can dear.

But people don't
Trust her,
For she is a woman,
And men don't care.

So she keeps her thoughts
Close to chest,
In diaries stained
By coffee spills.

One day maybe,
When people change.
Diaries and letters
With poems and plots

Will reach the ears,
Touch the eyes
Of readers and peers
Around the sphere.

One day, maybe.

"Puppeteer"

Lifting strings to play,
The little boy
Of a forgotten pianist
Of classical prowess.

Clicking the keys,
He was whipped to learn,
For failing is horror,
And horror is pain.

There is no pleasure
In the art of the song,
There is no beauty
In the tear of the skin.

Like a puppet on strings,
Lifting to ring the piano stings.
He doesn't play, he doesn't sing
He only lies limps for puppeteers.

A tortured artist,
A crying dove flying,
In the locked cage,
Of a puppeteer stage.

"Sore Eyes"

Disheveled hair,
Spittle dotted lips,
And messy button up;
The true sight for sore eyes.

I drag on a stick,
Trying to get a taste
In my cracked mouth,
Though nature is no friend.

I am a jester,
A clown,
A freak,
A lost vagabond.

I haven't a clue
Why I try,
Why I sing,
Why I write.

I am the sight for
Poor eyes,
Scorned eyes,
Sore eyes.

"Portrait of a Poet"

Dawned in black attire,
With ink dotted hands tired.
He has written through the night
Of spite and fights and
what's deemed right.

He fought for something final,
He fought so many could see,
A truth behind the masses
Of integrity and will.

Though censored he became,
When leaders thought it obscene,
He was maimed and beaten
By a society of dames.

It is easy to swing a view
With a simple word or two,
But this portrait of a poet
Does not reach to you.

It comes off as a whine
Of a man who can't be calmed,
A man throwing tantrum
When people don't sing his song.

The poet of illusion
Trying to trick a group,
For a common will
Of disenchanting thrill.

Though the quill he dawns tonight
Can be one's alibi,
If it proves to be a doom to all
And not one to save them.

The poet sees the world
How he wants to view it.
He writes to share a view
With people like all of you.

"Best in Show"

Sniff an asshole,
Piss on a hydrant,
Scream at a fellow,
Cry for a meal.

I am the god
Spelt backwards,
For every taller being
Worships my existence.

I am the best in show,
The best of all,
The best forever,
You damn losers.

-Dog

"Revolution Poem"

I was sentenced to a
1000 years of loneliness,
For persuading a view
through poetry new.

I did not know, my judge and juror
Were people of single eye.
It conflicts, it combats and
It obstructs what the free one's believe in.

So as I reside, in my
Hilltop prison. I look down
On all who opposed the new,
For old idea's askew.

When I am free, we take what
Is ours and what is
To be take by force, by choice
Never defy when it's time to choose.

May revolution be a wakeup,
To Lackeys and shit heads the same.
Times are a'changing and
People need replacing.

"The Gardener"

Sitting alone in a
Church yard Garden.
Francis puffs a cloud
Out a pipe he carries.

He spent his life
Growing into a man
Who would conquer
The world,

But now…

He sits by tulips
And violets in rows,
Ashamed even though
He creates beautiful scenes.
People come to the
Church to see
What Francis has created,
What is to be seen.

He cannot hear
The cheers for more,
He cannot understand
Why people care.

They are flowers,
Just flowers,
Will only and always
Only be flowers.

Minister Langley
Joins Francis on the bench,
He doesn't speak,
Just stares.

Rows upon rows,
Like an army marching,
Line the yard
Like a beautiful renegade.

"Why do you work here?"
"Because job hunting is shit."
"Why do you work here?"
"I told ya, job hunting, nothing else."

The minister doesn't
Look at Francis,
Even as Francis stares
In utter bewilderment.

A man who has watched
And never spoken to him,
Comes out of the blue
And sits with queries unanswerable.

"Look at the flowers."

"Why? Something wrong?"
"Look at the flowers."
"Fine," Francis looks straight.

"What do you see?"
"Flowers, lots of fucking flowers."
"What else?"
"Flowers, rows and rows of flowers."

"Harder, look Harder."
"Alright, am I missing something?"
"Look harder, Francis, look harder."
"Fine, I'll look 'harder'"

The gardener stares
And sees not much,
A tulip row
In front of others.

Each row was placed
In what Francis thought
Was a lackluster combination.
An asshole who should be fired.

"I see tulips,
In front of daisies,
Followed by lillies
Then violets."

"I see a pattern."
"Same here, it's called
Being uncreative."
The minister chuckled

"And what was last year?"
"Different?"
"Yes and I say very creative."
They finally locked eyes.

"A flower is what comes
And goes. It is born to be
Beautiful but leaves broken.
Though there is always a new year."

The gardener for once
Stayed silent,
Wasn't snarky,
Wasn't an ass.

"Francis, you are
The church flower.
People don't care for
A plant, you are the gift."

Tears dot the grass.
Francis was confused,
Why would he cry?
Why should he feel?

"Every year, you come
Different. You come changed.
An arrangement arrives,
And it stays because of you."

The minster places his hand
Atop Francis's and squeezes,
"You are the flower
You are the gift."

He stands and walks
Back to a service
He left for the gift.
Francis just stares.

Looking upon the yard,
Full of color,
Full of beauty,
Full of Francis.

He is a flower,
And who reads this is too.
You are perfect,
You are the gift.

"Ocarina"

A little vagabond
Travels town to town.
No shoes, only dress,
No coins, only music.

She plays a cracked
Tune out a teal ocarina,
A melody too sweet
For a world in defeat.

She tells the passers
She isn't lost,
She has a home,
The world to roam.

She plays the music
Too sweet to bare,
So lovely with care,
And no room for despair.

She once had a family,
Then the soldiers came,
And out they lay
In broken brown caskets.

She weeps in private
But hides behind a song,
For music is a defence
Where she remains at large.

The soldiers attack all
And blame it on the commies,
Though Natzi or not,
There stands moral will.

May this war end,
The first wasn't sparing.
I miss my friends and family,
But now I remain wandering.

"Truth or Dare"

I want you
to love me
As a loser,
And kill me
As a saint.

I want you to
Carry me to
Unknown lands,
For there I shall be
Maimed.

I want you to
Watch my soft
Body fall into
Earth and sing
A solemn tune.

I want you to be there my love,
I want you to be there.

I want you to
declare my name,
The prophet,
The hero
Of shame.

I want you to beware my love,
I want you to beware.

Fight me,
Kill me,
Love me,
Have me,

For nothing in life
Is fair my love,
When life is
Truth or dare.

"Study of a Model"

Who is she,
Who doesn't see beauty,
In the angel
That she is.

A model,
Stand upon
The pedestal
Of a painter who watches.

He analyzes
The curves of her waist,
The tone of her neck,
And the beauty spots
On her thigh.

She only watches
Him scribble then paint,
Where she thought she would
Look like a Medusa.

She isn't ready,
She cannot bare,
To see horror of
A stranger, defining
Her beauty is due to her body.

Jackson Durocher

She cannot bare,
While exposed above
In a rugged dress,
With a breast to share.

The painter looks up
And mutters 'perfect,'
Then turns the canvas
To the girl who spins
And faces the door.

"Is something up my dear?"
"Please; don't stare."
"Okay, fix your dress,
Take your time. I am
Here when you are ready."

She adjusts the top.
Take 3 inner breathes
Then out blow two.
Turn, face, walk, stare.

The painting…
It is normal,
It is ideal.
'How am I not ugly?'

Doubt,
The killer of beauty,
The assassin of confidence,
And the anxiety of the unknown.

The painter softly speaks,
And reminds her
She is complete,
In beauty,
In grace,
In the face of others.

The study of a model,
And the anxiety they face,
The horror of unknown,
With their body to show.
May all angels
See their worth,
In the painting,
Or photo
Of an artist.

"The Dancer"

The little dancer in blue
Does a leap for the audience,
Observing her mood and how
She may swoon all the watchers.

She has practiced,
She has condition,
And she has honed
What she thought perfect.

She puts her worth on the dance,
As backup matches routine,
And people stare at her,
Like a little music box
Lulling a baby to sleep.

She has dreamed of being a dancer,
A little ballerina,
On swan lake being
All the audience takes.

She longs to be in the spotlight,
To feel warmth in a stage light,
Though her peers no longer
Follow and now they dance in sync,
To something didn't think possible.

They changed routine to a different piece
She never learn, they abandoned her in
Light of a crowd audience pondering
If the abrupt unfamiliarity is part of the show.
The dancer grows panicked, not knowing what to do.

She improvising, trying to match,
Trying to save what is already lost.
The music speeds and dancer grow fast,
She turns and turns and turns and turns
Then…awake

In a cold sweat, at home in bed,
Alone to ponder,
Alone to think,
Is she worth it?
Is it nerves?
Will she fail?
Will she succeed?

Staring at the dress
She longed to wear,
Until a tear forms
And questions swarm.

Jackson Durocher

A picture of mom,
Beautiful in black,
As a swan on swan lake,
In years before her.

A whisper forms from somewhere
Near, like an angel from above;
It sounds like her mom.

Whispers of bravery,
Whispers of love,
Whispers of courage,
Whispers from above.

She smiles and cries
Then stare in her eyes of a mirror,
Telling herself 'you can do this'
She will be 'the dancer'

The show went well,
She was thrown a rose
Or two and sworn she will
Be a swan of swan lake.

This is for you, mom.

"Bitch Please"

I am assaulted with words
Of some rather awful discord,
I am told I hurt the feelings
Of a lady I haven't known.

I swear she has me mistaken,
I swear I mean no pain,
But she keeps the verbal hand
Striking across my rough face.

I try to get in a word,
Though foot in mouth I go,
For when silence took hold,
I spoke these fateful words;

"Bitch please!"

"Another Hug"

Sarah and Walter
Beggars in the last book,
Now have feet in the door
Of providence and shelter.

A year of picking pocketing,
They have themselves a home,
A little shack of oak
In a corner of the town.

Walter tries to work,
Live as an honest man.
Sarah goes to school,
And earn an honest life.

Though habits are still there,
For both of them return
With dollars and bills,
From wallets swiped today.

Sarah finds school boring,
She'd rather be on the streets.
Walter gets fired after
Just one week of work.

Sarah wants the home,
Where Walter and her roamed.
Not being false saints in
A world that ain't theirs.

Sarah throws a book,
At the teachers face,
And gets herself expelled
To where she skips with glee.

Walter comes homes,
To warn of his decision,
And Sarah comforts with
A choice she had made.

Honesty is not a must,
For those who work in dust,
Swiping and begging,
When you trust in life on whim.

Sarah hugs Walter and
Walters holds her tight,
She takes his hand
And they walked then run

To the town of possibility,
As father and daughter should see,
They will pay the bill of their shack
With the jobs they know best.

Sarah and Walter,
Beggars and family
Forevermore.

"Stranger"

The stranger
Stares blankly,
Distantly,
Absently.

He is lost,
Though my hotel
Looks like a home so
He deserves a visit.

Standing under
A street lamp,
He sprints into
The lobby

I do not know
The man,
And he doesn't
Know me.

But we shared
A stare and
Now aware that
I need to now beware.

I am the second floor,
He is stomping up
The stairs and into
My hall.

123,
456,
789,
Now he is here.

Bang,
Bang,
Bang,
Let him in.

Crash,
Pow,
Bam,
He knocked down the door.

Wow,
Wow,
He loves what you've done
With the place.

The stranger,
The critic,
The loyal,
The friend.

"Family"

A word,
A group,
A bond,
A place.

Family is what got my book published,
Family is what kept me going.
Family is something you cannot buy,
But I know I have won the best.
My father, the photographer,

The man who captured life.
The one who gave me strength,
And the one I idol most.

My mother, the cheerleader,
The lady who gave me faith.
The one who believes,
And never doubts for a second.

My brother, the artist.
The guy who paints,
And creates a bond;
The guy I relate to the most.

My sister, the beauty,
The one who knows she's loved,
By the family,
By the boyfriend,
By everyone.

The dogs, the loyalty.
The ones who bring all cheer,
The ones who save,
The people the dogs most needed.

Family is beauty,
And mine is most precious.

"Goodbye, My Love, Goodbye"

Lying all alone,
In a bed you'd occupy,
I feel your arms around me,
Like a phantom touch of mine.

It hasn't been a year and
Eyes are still not dry,
As I said at your deathbed,
"Goodbye, my love, goodbye."

I promised you I'd be strong
But that has not been the case,
As I pace and stew and wonder,
How you could ever be in my place.

I miss you my darling,
I miss you my love,
I miss you so much honey,
And I know I long for you.

Baxter, our dog,
He cuddles me at night,
A presence to get me to sleep,
When I know I'd rather weep.

Why would you leave my love,

I hate to have you gone.
We vowed 'til death do we part,'
But death came way too soon.

My love, I miss you,
My love, please come home,
My love, I need you,
My love, I want you.

Though I know my wish is fraught,
And I will not have my way,
So I write this poem to say my claim
In dotted ink of pain.

"Goodbye, my love, Goodbye,"
I'll stay strong for you.
I'll try a happy tune.
"Goodbye, my love, goodbye."

"Persuasion"

Fly me to the planet of persuasion,
Tell me what people say about me.

I know I'm not the cunning,
I know I'm not the brave.

I'm just the clever asshole,
You declare me to be.

So please please please fly me to persuasion.

So please please please fly me to persuasion.

I have not much to offer to the vagabond with me,

While we cross the river Styx with no offer to the dead.

So please join me to persuasion,
Please let me take you to persuasion.

I haven't a clue,
How I'm supposed to reach for you.

With each word that I spill,
Coming to you without noise.

So please open up to persuasion,
So please let me convince you of persuasion.

Last night I came home,
And locked myself away,

Like a captive in a tower,
Whose owner is himself.

So please let me be free from persuasion,
Please unshackle me from persuasion .

I told you I want out of this,
Unholy game we play.
Where the dealer only cares for the bet I lay to claim.

Please pay me out of my persuasion,
Please let me pay off my persuasion.

Did you know my mother called
And persuaded me to stay,

For you are the only one who
Puts up with all my shame.

So please convince everyone of persuasion,
Please hold dear our persuasion.
I only want your persuasion,
I only deserve your persuasion,
I only need your persuasion.

"Boy in the Red Vest"

The boy in the red vest,
Was no boy;
Instead someone who
Looked rather masculine.

Boys and girls would
Refer to her as Jay;
The boyish girlish name
Suited for the one who appeared both.

Jay, who's real name smeared
Like a message on a palm,
Is unknown for she has
Accepted the tease given.

Walking down a downtown
Crossroad, an older woman
Called out to her.
'Hey miss! Hey miss, help me here!'

Jay ignored for why would
Someone refer to her correctly?
"Hey Miss! Help me please!"
Turning for shits and giggles, they met eyes.

Jay raised a finger
Pointed towards herself.
"I don't see any other women?"
Jay trotted over.

The woman was wheelchair bound,
With a cast on her left lower arm;
Unable to wheel herself quickly
Across the busy street.

Panicked rose and she called to
The nearest woman she saw.
Jay was the lucky one and
The lady was fortunate.

Jay wheeled her across the street,
Up on pavement where
The lady offered repayment
Which was greatly refused.

"How did you know I was female?"
"What do you mean?"
"Aren't I boyish looking"
"But aren't you female?

Jay froze and thought,
Ponder and queried,
Her idea of objectivity
Of Jay being female.

"I am…a girl" came out slowly."
"I am… a girl, always a girl."
"I am… Jay, I am… Catrice,"
"I am a girl, I am Catrice."

The woman was staring
While revolutions took hold,
She wasn't judging,
Just was curious of this girl.

A girl named Catrice,
A girl renamed Jay,
A girl forced living as a boy,
Even when a girl was true to herself.

She wasn't trans
Though support she did,
For she lived both lives
And commend those who strut proud.

Catrice hugged the woman
And ran towards her home,
Where she told her roommate
Her name is Catrice.

Catrice and always Catrice.
Once Jay and learned from Jay.
Loving herself for two personalities,
The masculine and feminine.

"Neon"

Keep me warm
On nights most cold,
Holding hands down
neon streets.

Signs blare,
Drawing passers near,
To buildings of ill-will,
Buildings of faltered folly.

Step with me
In walking rhythm,
As neon stares
in utter dare.

"Do you trust?"
"Do what you must?"
Bare pink legs and
A flashing stout.

My lover stares
then looks away,
For her avoidance
Keeps me at bay.

Hand in hand,
Trapping warmth
In grip, we take a trip
Down neon streets bare.

"Totoro"

The tree grows far
Upon the grassy plain
Of natures painting
Of serenity.

The woody lands
All cupped in hands
Of protection by a
Deity, a friend, an ally.

Totoro,
The neighbour and friend,
Bringing beauty
And sharing grace.

He watches upon
Chimney tops and
Up on trees at the
Village below.

The fields of workers,
The children trekking to school,
And lovers, sweet lovers,
Shelter during a storm.

Totoro watches,
Totoro stares,
Totoro smiles,
Totoro cares.

For rain brings rebirth
And gives the flowers a drink
As two hide under a roof covered altar of the
Buddha praying for two.

They offer a coin and
pray to each other,
The boy to see mom again,
And the girl to stay brave.

Totoro though invisible,
For no one sees a spirit,
Especially one of nature,
Especially one of cheer.

Offers up a leaf,
When the two are gone,
To bring good luck to the lovers,
Though they'll always have each other.

"Sleeping Mother"

A mother is tired
And sleeping softly,
After a night of jobs
And prepping meals for
Loved ones tomorrow.

She curls arms crossed,
As a pillow to cushion her
Head softly to slumber,
To count the sheep,
To fall deep asleep.

The night before she
Was one to defend,
A lady of the night,
A force to be wary.

Mom the fighter,
Mom the assassin,
Mom the contracted,
Mom the killer.

She swiftly took down
Crooks and king pins
Who spin crime.
She follows and controls
Those who harm the weakened.

Mom has taken bruises,
Mom has been swiped,
Mom has been beaten,
But creams and foundation,
Are easy to play alibi's.

Color surrounds
The beauty of the mom
Who sleeps so tired
While loved ones smile wide.
The sleeping hero of my own home.

I love you mom.

"Hades and Persephone"

Born for dead,
Born for nature.

Rules the end,
Creates a beginning.

A yin and yang,
A good and evil.

Within each other,
Love did blossom.

Among the seeds of doubt.

Married and both rule
Of a land thought bare.

A wife creating beauty
Only seems fair.

Hades and Persephone.

Rule long, rule fair
And always be there for each other.

"Kings Bride"

"Are you sure about this?"
"Yes, I believe I am."
"If you insist."
He places a hand
Upon shoulder so thin.

"He will be cruel,"
"I know."
"He will be of wrongful will,"
"I know."
"He has killed prior wives."

She knows all of this king,
He of his tyranny
Of those who died,
And those who survived.

But she must stay strong,
For father to live,
So riches can cure,
The sickness within him.

To save a man by wedding
Is sad but poetic still,
She will be bride to hell
And wife to the devil's name.

"I trust your choice,"
"Thank you sir."
"I commend your courage
May you live forevermore,"

Tomorrow she is wed,
And may be dead,
If she doesn't produce what
The king desires. A son.

(Henry VIII)
(The Mad King)

"A Portrait of a Daughter"

A daughter of a vagabond
Though raised in higher class,
Since mother remarried
And dad left so soon.

Her new Dad is a banker
Who owns a few good places
But she never knew her father
Was oh so near.

Her 12th birthday,
Father came to see
How his girl has grown,
The one who shares his name.

Cake and presents surrounds
The girl bewildered staring,
At who this homeless man is,
Drinking punch alone.

Walking to drink with him,
She asked his title and name,
To which he responds
"The name, none; the title, father."

Dropping her glass,

She exclaimed in denial,
"My dad is dead."
"Well I am alive right now ain't I."

"Prove it… please,"
"Birthmark, under left thigh."
Either he's a creep
Or he's her father.

"What's my prior full name?"
"Dalia Langley O'Donald."
"Dad…really?"
He goes in for a hug.

But before arms wrap around,
She knees him in the groin.
"Why would you leave?
Why would you go?"

"Because I was selfish,
And because I was scared."
"That's not enough,"
"And it never will be, I know."

She pondered,
She stewed,
Did not know what to do,
Will she forgive? Or forget?

Her stepdad is an ass,
Her real one is a flake,
Her mother is overzealous,
And she feels like a mistake.

Daniella, Mother,
See's that the dad is here,
Pissed and angered,
She marches like a soldier scorned.

"Why are you here?
Why must you come?
Why not stay away?
Why not leave things be?"

He wants to tell the mother,
'She's my daughter too'
But he's silenced by a tone,
And told to just go home.

Refusing to cause a scene,
Appearing all obscene,
He walked himself
To the door, until…

"Wait!" Pierced the crowd
Of a daughter yelling aloud.
"Don't go, not yet…Dad."
A smile came to his face.

The mother objects,
But abstained anyway,
For a daughters interrogation
Of fatherhood abandonment.

No apologies,
No gifts,
No forgiveness,
Cannot fix

The hole,
The piece,
Missing from
A lost relationship.

But acceptance
Somehow remains,
A new chapter
Two can play.

The daughter
Takes the man,
The sudden dad
To allow a choice.

To be,
Or not to be,
The father
To the daughter.

She is opening her heart
To potential break,
And risking her joy
For a sense of normalcy.

But what is normalcy?
A made up phrase,
To play an idea of
What is abnormal.

To have a dad is normal,
But to not have one is too,
She chose her normal
And you can too.

"New Orleans"

Take me down to
New Orleans.
Find me a place where
No one's been.

I've torn my jacket,
I've worn my shoes,
Trying to find what happened
To you.

Martha my darling,
Martha my musée;
Take me back to gambling
Where I'll sing blues.

Fill my cup,
Take out the tray,
Where cold shivers seize
My days.

Mother was baker,
Father was a con,
Trading his voice for
Dollars on a card.

Father skipped town,
Mother was afraid,
That people he dealt
Would take me away.

I'm taking the train,
To the place most alone,
Where letter never come
And pigeons never fly.

Martha come and find me,
Martha here I am,
Living my days
With dust and sand.

In New Orlean,
Where the law has
Blindfolds
Screaming damn in our hands.

Mother has moved on,
She found herself a man,
One to protect,
One to serve.

Father turned up broken,
Wet from head to toe,
Bourbon on breath,
Cigarette smeared palms.

Martha I am lonely,
Martha I have no home,
Martha come save me,
Martha I am scared.

Mother stood up,
To the bastard at the door.
But poor old me,
I am like my old man.

Martha stay away,,
I am not to be swayed,
I am a jester,
And con of emotions.

New Orleans burns,
And boils like a pot over fire.
I am sweating my crimes away.
I will be home soon a new man.

Stay strong darling,
Stay strong Martha.

"The Animals and the Girl"

A one way dog door
And a girl locked in a parlour.
She is alone except for
9 animals accompanying her sorrow.

One fish with two hamsters,
One cat and two dogs,
And a soft brown ferret
Playing with two silk bunny's.

She should feel sad?
She should feel trapped?
Being shackled in isolation,
With only creatures playing friendly faces?

She actually feels quite happy
With her pets of mercy,
Playing friends in her
Room she calls home.

Everyday, at 10am,
Food slides through
The doggy door,
With a meal for pets and little girls.

They all run over and

Slobber down the meal.
Little girl stares,
Little girl squeals

They all seem viscous
Snapping up their food,
But something in it's desperate
Like they all have something to lose.

The little girl watches,
Then joins the frenzy feast,
And tries to grab what she can eat,
Though she only gets few treats.

By the time the feeding is done,
And nothings on their plates,
They go back to the mundane life,
They live inside this room.

The hamsters run on wheels,
The bird flies around,
The cats and dogs bicker,
And fur balls all slack off.

They only one unmention
Is the fish she soon calls
Bubbles for the bubbles he
Blows when nothing is shown.

The girl grows fond of
her family of pets,
Her companion in confinement
By unknown secret captors.

She spends all her days,
From 7 to 16 as a prisoner
In a parlour of a mansion
Down by the coast.

Until one meal,
they shared together,
Laced with secret meds
In bread they were fed.

They all fell asleep,
Into a deep slumber,
And awoke on a freight car
Of a train going south.

Released into a world
They have not known,
They don't know what to do
They only know the door.

The door that feeds
Every 10am
Where will they be fed?
How will they eat?

They will learn from
A mystery,
A world unknown
But together they'll rise.

Like the companions
Growing together.

"Ocean of Words"

An ocean of words
Separates my future
With the present.
I am not moses
Or a captain;
I'm just one with Jack
And an untuned Ukulele

"Self-Love Discovered"

I wrote beauty,
Created grace,
Defined a future
In an reliable place.

I made a home
Where soldiers drum,
A lullaby and not
A battle cry.

I persuaded a man
To hold a hand
Of an old lady
Across the street.

I sewed a quilt
Of past self's guilt,
Where I have built
A new world at will.

I am the author,
I am the son,
I am the poet,
I am the one.

I was created by love
And gained a family,
With a sibling young,
  And a sibling old.

I earned three dogs,
And then three more,
  A grandfather,
And a grandmother.

I travelled the world
With people held dear,
And stories of cheer,
  We share all year.

I am the fortunate,
I am the lucky,
I am the worthy,
I am Jackson Durocher.

Afterword

Hi everyone, this is Jackson Durocher talking!

I want to thank everyone who has picked up this book, it truly has been special writing it. I planned to take writing slow, to have some time to contemplate each idea though soon they all came flooding through and I did not stop. I have received so much love and praise that I never thought I'd receive. I first published my first book (Poetry in a half-shell) with the idea of a title of Author and nothing else. The thrill I received when reviews came in, I knew I wanted a book 2. I decided to stay on an animal theme and created the title from rhyming my favourite animal (Bear.)

My family helped me with the editing and critiques of this volume and I do feel it is better than my prior collection.

To whoever reads this blurb of excited will, Thank you,

Thank you so much for reading. I truly am so lucky to have so many beautiful people in my life. I love you all!

P.S. Throughout this book, there has been paintings and sketches done, most from history, The rest from someone dear who prefers to remain anonymous.

To the anonymous, thank you so much and I truly look up to you as a person and friend.

About the Author

Jackson was born in 2003 and grew up in Alberta, Canada even as he wrote this book.

He was always an artsy kid, growing up playing 6 instruments and getting into partner dancing (Lindy, Ballroom, Latin, Country, etc.) And trying his best to dabble in sketching.

He is currently enrolled in Child and Youth Care and working as a Youth Worker. He has always been fascinated in the ideas and effects of Trauma on the brain. In his 4th year, he hopes to go into an analytical and supportive role in the children's mental health sector.

Hopefully he can make it but life is funny with mysterious twists and discoveries.